WIMBLEDON T

(A Fascinating Book Containing Wimbledon Tennis Facts, Trivia, Images & Memory Recall Quiz: Suitable for Adults & Children)

By

Matthew Harper

Image Courtesy of shu

For legal reasons we are obliged to state the following:

Copyright 2014 Matthew Harper

ISBN-13: 978-1500269531

ISBN-10: 1500269530

All rights reserved. No reproduction, copying or transmission of this publication, CD's or DVD included in this system may be made without written permission. No paragraph of this publication may be reproduced, copied or transmitted without written permission, or in accordance with the Copyright Act 1956 (amended).

Hi and a very warm welcome to "Wimbledon Tennis".

I'm one of those people who loves to hear about extraordinary facts or trivia about anything. They seem to be one of the few things my memory can actually recall. I'm not sure if it's to do with the shock or the "WoW" factor but for some reason my brain seems to store at least some of it for a later date.

I've always been a great believer in that whatever the subject, if a good teacher can inspire you and hold your attention, then you'll learn! Now I'm not a teacher but the system I've used in previous publications on Amazon seems to work well, particularly with children.

This "Wimbledon Tennis" edition includes a selection of those "WoW" facts combined with some pretty awesome pictures, if I say so myself! At the end there is a short "True or False" quiz to check memory recall and to help cement some of the information included in the book. Don't worry though, it's a bit of fun but at the same time, it helps to check your understanding.

Please note that if you're an expert on this subject then you may not find anything new here. If however you enjoy hearing sensational and extraordinary trivia and you like looking at some great pictures, then I think you'll love it.

Matt.

In true Matthew Harper tradition, I thought that before we get down to some of those amazing facts, we might begin with a few interesting snapshots, just to get the juices flowing..............

ROGER FEDERER

Image Courtesy of toga

RAFAEL NADAL

Image Courtesy of SJByles

PETE SAMPRAS

Image Courtesy of theomin

SERENA WILLIAMS

Image Courtesy of Boss Tweed

JIMMY CONNORS

Image Courtesy of robbiesaurus

BJORN BORG

Image Courtesy of MadMarlin

MARTINA NAVRATILOVA

Image Courtesy of robbiesaurus

BORIS BECKER

Image Courtesy of MST77

CHRIS EVERT

Image Courtesy of Florida Memory

JOHN MCENROE

Image Courtesy of dbking

Okay, that's it for the warm up, let's get on with the game......

Image Courtesy of nicubunu

Did you know that of all the Grand Slam tennis tournaments, Wimbledon is the only one that's played on grass?

Image Courtesy of Carine06

Did you know that Wimbledon first began all the way back in 1877 and that the location itself is a suburb of London?

Image Courtesy of ozziebackpacker

Did you know that the Ladies Single Championship was introduced as early as 1884?

Did you know that Wimbledon always begins six weeks before the first Monday of August?

Image Courtesy of Steve F

Did you know that the trophy issued to the ladies champion is called the Venus Rosewater Dish?

Image Courtesy of Pavel Lebeda / Česká sportovní

Did you know that Martina Navratilova has won the ladies championship a record nine times more than any other player to date?

Image Courtesy of robbiesaurus

Did you know that the youngest player ever to win a Wimbledon singles event was Charlotte Dod at the tender age of 15 years old in 1887?

Did you know that a wooden tennis racket was used for the last time at Wimbledon in 1987?

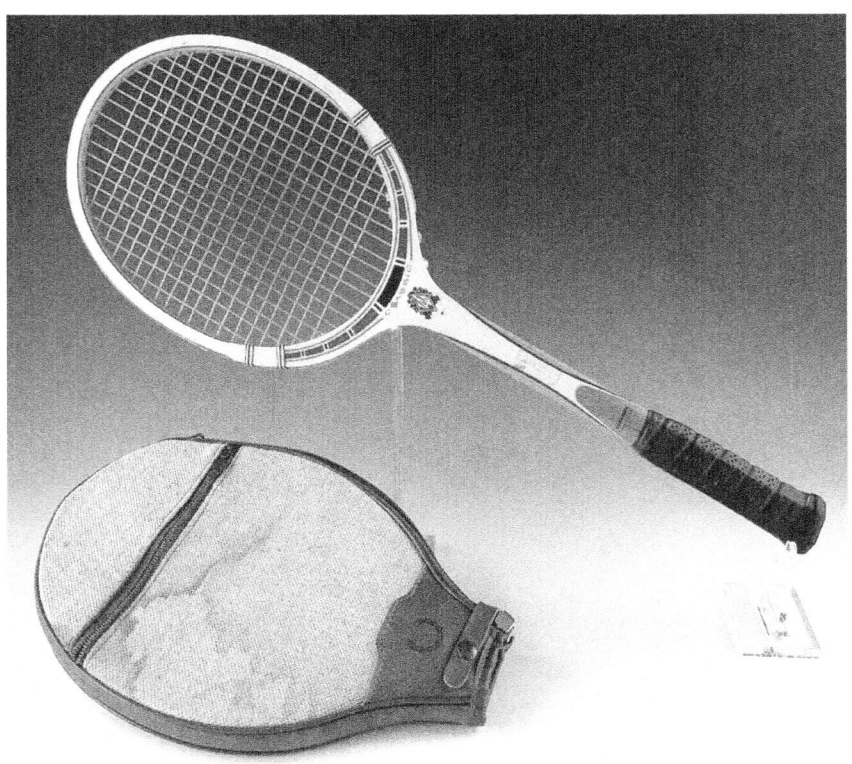

Did you know that about 300,000 tea/coffee drinks were sold during Wimbledon in 2013?

Image Courtesy of Carine06

Did you know that during World War II, a bomb destroyed the center court at Wimbledon?

Did you know that the first ever winner of Wimbledon, (that wasn't from Europe), was May Sutton when she won the championship for the US in 1905?

Did you know that the first black player to win the ladies championship was Althea Gibson in 1957?

Did you know that Spencer Gore won the first Wimbledon men's singles championship and the match only lasted 48 minutes?

Did you know that the youngest male player to win the championship was Boris Becker at the age of 17?

Image Courtesy of KTC

Did you know that the grass used in the Wimbledon courts is cut exactly to 8mm in height?

Image Courtesy of Carine06

Did you also know that the type of grass used in the courts is made of 100% ryegrass?

Image Courtesy of Forest & Kim Starr

Did you know that the electronic system used at Wimbledon to determine the trajectory of the ball is called Hawk-Eye?

. Image Courtesy of JukoFF

Did you know that 757 players (including qualifiers) competed in the 2013 tournament?

Image Courtesy of laobc

Did you know that the Queen of England has attended Wimbledon four times in her history, 1957, 1962, 1977 and 2010?

Image Courtesy of Michael Gwyther-Jones

Did you know that it takes 6,000 staff to run the Wimbledon tournament including 250 ball boys and girls?

Image Courtesy of ShotHotspot.com

Did you know that full, life, honorary and temporary are the names of the different types of membership available at Wimbledon?

Image Courtesy of Mvkulkarni23

Did you know that Venus Williams currently holds the record for the fastest ladies serve at a record 207.6 km/h (129.0 mph)?

Image Courtesy of Julie Edgley

Did you know that the roof at Wimbledon is used if the wind speed reaches 43 miles per hour? It takes 10 minutes to close!

Image Courtesy of Carine06

Did you know that yellow balls were first introduced to the tournament in 1986?

Image Courtesy of Vladsinger

Did you know that around 30,000 kilos of fresh strawberries will be consumed every year at the Wimbledon event?

Image Courtesy of Magnus D

Did you know that approximately 40,000 tennis balls will be used over the course of the tournament?

Image Courtesy of rickydiver78

Did you know that Wimbledon has a capacity for 38,500 people?

Image Courtesy of anonlinegreenworld

Did you know that prize money was first introduced to the tournament in 1968 where it amounted to only £25,000 ($42,500 USD approx)?

Image Courtesy of Benjamí Villoslada i Gil

Did you know that white must be worn by all players throughout the tournament?

Image Courtesy of Carine06

Did you know that the ball boys and girls are referred to as BBG's?

Image Courtesy of Chris Eason

Did you know that Wimbledon refuses to sponsor any form of advertising around its courts?

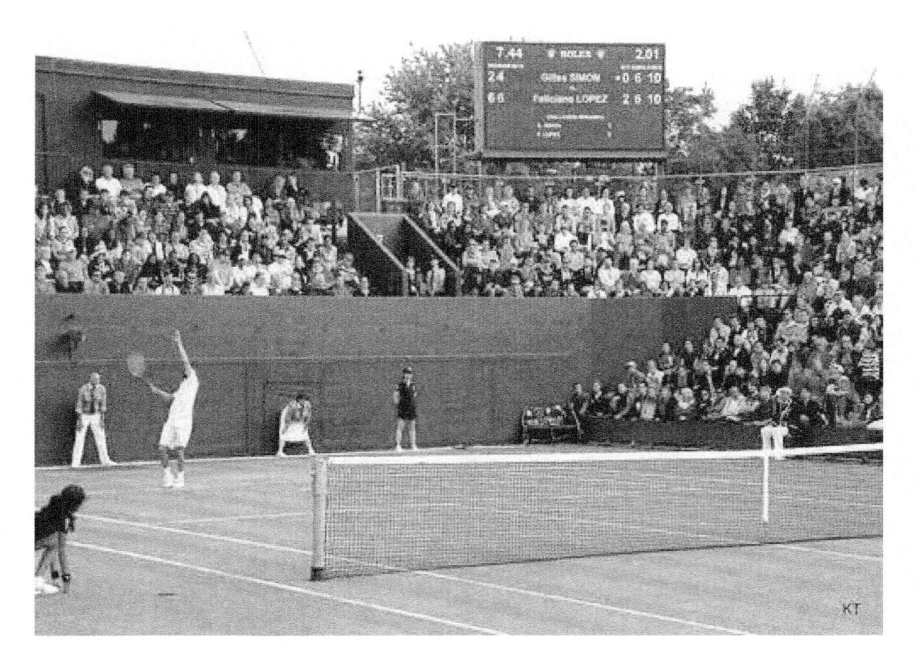

Image Courtesy of Carine06

Did you know that the Sunday half way through the event is traditionally still used as a formal day of rest in the tournament?

Image Courtesy of Arvin61r58

Did you know that Tim Henman, in 1995, became the first player ever to be disqualified for losing his temper?

Image Courtesy of internetsense

Did you know that it was only as recently as 2007, that the prize money for both male and female players was equalized? Venus Williams was the first lady to benefit from the new ruling.

Image Courtesy of Tim Schofield

Did you know that the youngest player to compete at Wimbledon was Mita Klima of Austria in 1907? She was only thirteen!

Men's doubles final, Wimbledon 1907

Did you know that the winner of the first men's championship, Spencer Gore, once commented that Wimbledon was a "bit boring"? "How times have changed"!

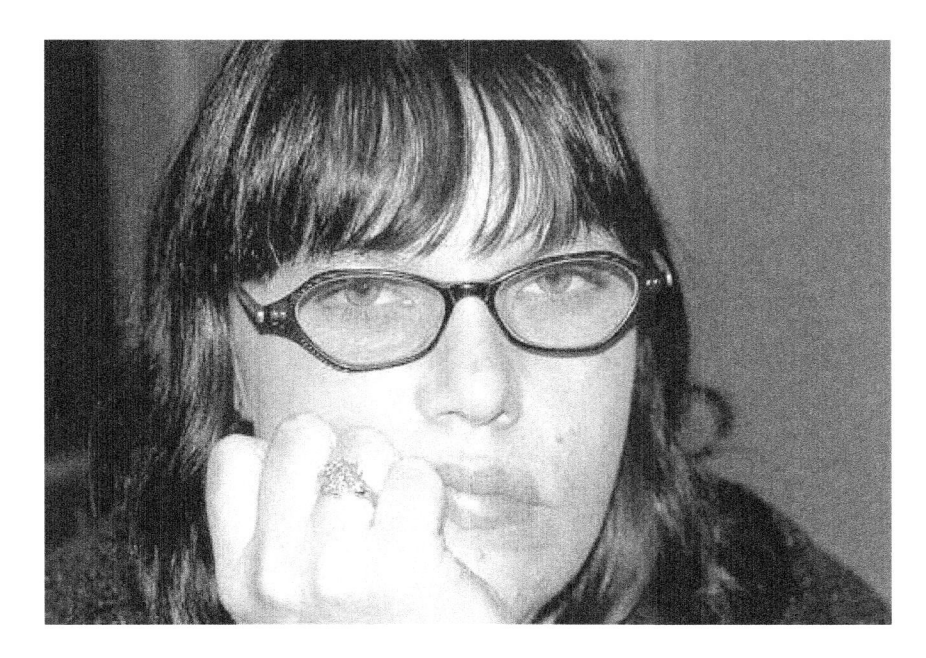

Image Courtesy scragz

Did you know that Wimbledon is actually the oldest tennis tournament in existence and was originally set up to help pay for croquet equipment?

PALL-MALL.

Did you know that since 1922, the Wimbledon tournament has been based at Church Road but the original location was at Worple Road? Growing popularity for the event forced the club to move to larger premises.

Wimbledon at Worple Road

Did you know that the first televised broadcast of the championship was held during the 1937 tournament by the BBC?

Image Courtesy of Tim Loudon

Did you know that the Wimbledon center court is also now used as an Olympic venue?

Image Courtesy of BaldBoris

Did you know that the average age of a ball boy or girl is fifteen years of age and that they're only chosen from schools in select London boroughs?

Image Courtesy of Chris Eason

Did you know that the double's events were first introduced in 1884?

Image Courtesy of Bo Mertz

Did you know that the queue for fans used to obtain seats at Wimbledon is actually called "The Queue"?

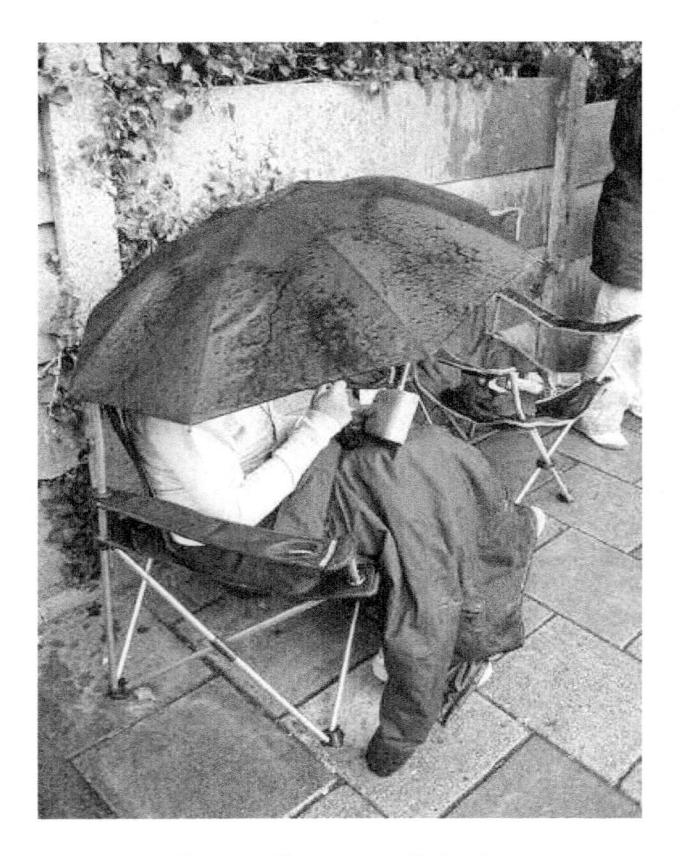

Image Courtesy of elyob

Did you know that "Slazenger" is the main contributor of tennis balls for the Wimbledon tournament?

Image Courtesy of Tennis-Bargains.com

Did you know that until Andy Murray won the men's championship in 2013, it had been 77 years (1936) since another British man, Fred Perry, had won the men's singles title?

Did you know that the hill used by spectators outside the center court to watch on the big screen is nicknamed "Henman Hill"?

Image Courtesy of Matt Morelli

Did you know that a hawk by the name of Rufus is employed to protect the center court from pigeons and works from 5.30pm to 9.30pm?

Image Courtesy of Catherine Wright

Did you know that the only wildcard to win Wimbledon's men's singles title was the Croat, Goran Ivanisevic in 2001?

Image Courtesy of daramot

Did you know that at Wimbledon in 1998, a match between Yevgeny Kafelnikov and Mark Philippoussis was interrupted by a mouse running onto the court?

Did you know that in 1957, Maria de Amorin from Brazil, managed 17 consecutive double-faults during one match?

Image Courtesy of Bo Mertz

That's about it for the trivia for now. I'd like to finish this publication with TEN "True or False" questions based on what you've just read. It should help you to really cement the information and to test your memory recall!..
....

DON'T FORGET TO KEEP YOUR SCORE: THERE'S 1 POINT FOR EACH OF THE FIRST 9 QUESTIONS AND 5 POINTS FOR THE BONUS QUESTION GIVING A TOTAL OF 14 POINTS ....

1.

TRUE or FALSE: Wimbledon always begins six weeks before the first Monday of August.

TRUE.

2.

TRUE or FALSE: The trophy issued to the ladies champion is called the Serena Rosewater Dish.

FALSE

The trophy issued to the ladies champion is called the **VENUS** Rosewater Dish.

3.

TRUE or FALSE: The first black player to win the ladies championship was Althea Gibson in 1857.

FALSE

The first black player to win the ladies championship was Althea Gibson in **1957**.

4.

TRUE or FALSE: The electronic system used at Wimbledon to determine the trajectory of the ball is called Birds-Eye.

FALSE

The electronic system used at Wimbledon to determine the trajectory of the ball is called **HAWK**-Eye.

5.

TRUE or FALSE: Wimbledon has a capacity for 38,500 people.

TRUE

6.

TRUE or FALSE: The ball boys and girls are referred to as BBC's.

FALSE

The ball boys and girls are referred to as **BBG's**.

7.

TRUE or FALSE: Tim Henman, in 1995, became the first player ever to be disqualified for losing his racket.

FALSE

Tim Henman, in 1995, became the first player ever to be disqualified for losing his **TEMPER**.

8.

TRUE or FALSE: The double's events were first introduced in 1884.

TRUE

9.

TRUE or FALSE: A hawk by the name of Rufus is employed to protect the center court from pigeons.

TRUE

10.

BONUS ROUND WORTH 5 POINTS

TRUE or FALSE: In 1957, Maria de Amorin from Brazil, managed 17 consecutive double-faults during one match.

TRUE

Congratulations, you made it to the end!

I sincerely hope you enjoyed my little Wimbledon Tennis project and that you learnt a thing or two. I certainly did when I was doing the research.

ADD UP YOUR SCORE NOW.

1 point for each of the first 9 correct answers plus 5 points for the bonus round giving a grand total of 14 points.

If you genuinely achieved 14 points then you are indeed a

"WIMBLEDON TENNIS MASTER".

8 to 13 points proves you are a

"WIMBLEDON TENNIS LEGEND".

4 to 7 points shows you are a

"WIMBLEDON TENNIS ENTHUSIAST".

0 to 3 points shows you are a

"WIMBLEDON TENNIS ADMIRER".

NICE WORK!

Matt.

Thank you once again for choosing this publication. If you enjoyed it then please let me know using the Customer Review Section through Amazon.

If you would like to read more of my work then simply type in my name using the Amazon Search Box and hopefully you'll find something else that "takes your fancy" or go directly to my website printed below.

Until we meet again,

Matthew Harper

www.matthewharper.info

Image Courtesy of shu

Printed in Great Britain
by Amazon